The Veterans Poems
Volume Two

Created by
Amber Guymer-Hosking

HEALING WITH WORD

We Will Remember Them

F ▽ G
FILM VOLT GROUP

Published By
Film Volt Group
Company Number **11833932**

Contents

Amber Guymer-Hosking

 Charity Ambassador of Help4HomelessVeterans and a veteran of the British Armed forces, Amber served for 11 years before becoming medically discharged for PTSD in 2016 in turn.

Amber became homeless Living out of her car and in hotels before Help 4 Homeless Veterans helped her and her young son to get off the streets of the UK.

Since becoming an Ambassador to help other Veterans get their lives back on a stable path and support for their PTSD.

Amber has now become a stable shining light for many Veterans not only in the UK but Internationally by telling her story on Podcasts and in Magazines to help create awareness for the many of the Veterans that are still to this day living on our streets or struggling to cope with life out of the armed forces.

Still suffering from the traumatic effects of PTSD Amber still feels the side effects of it all from time to time as it will never leave her.

The Veterans Poems is dedicated to those who are still out there feeling abandoned
after serving their country and still suffering from the traumatic events they have witnessed in their time.

"Sometimes the battle is hard and sometimes I have nearly thrown my own towel in because I wanted the pain to stop, though when this happens I have my own heroes, my son, my siblings, and the support of the people around me. "
"They give me strength"
"Amber Guymer-Hosking"

Special Thanks

I would like to thank all of my siblings for their continued support through my bad and good days. James, Johnny, Miles, Georgina and my son Brandon and my Nephew Charles Henry you're all my heroes. Thank you to my Mother, Grandparents for their continued support.

Thank you to all my family for being here for me on all occasions and fully supporting me in my endeavors and being my confidantes. And to many friends who have been amazing throughout my journey.

I would like to give my thanks to a wonderful charity, that supported me and my son through Homelessness because, without them, I would not be here now.

Help4HomelessVeterans Charity. Tom Wood and his beautiful wife Jean the founders and Steven Bentham-Bates their CEO, along with all of the other colleagues of Help4HomelessVeterans - you are all earth angels and deserve absolute credit for helping Veterans find safety and stability in a home.

I would like to thank you for making me one of your Ambassadors.

I am privileged to be an Ambassador of such a wonderful cause.

Along with a massive thank you for giving me your continued support for the last five years and a lifelong friendship.

I would also like to thank Kate Blewett for the support and opportunities she has given Brandon and me and is now a lifelong friend.

I would also like to give a massive thank you to Mark Busby for creating the front cover, but also for the opportunity and continued support he has given me throughout the last year and your friendship.

I would also like to give thanks to the Veterans Foundation for their continued support of me and charities around our Country.
Now, I would be remiss if I did not thank our British heroes and those who have served for the HM Forces and those who continue to serve for our belated Queen and our new King.

Thank you to those who have put their lives on the line for our Country.
Thank you to our Nation's Heroes.
Thank you to our Veterans and civilians who have sent me their personal heart felt poems.

A Look Inside The Minds Of Our Veterans

A Look Inside The Minds Of Our Veterans.

A look inside the mind of our surviving Military Veterans across the United Kingdom.

Perhaps you see their injuries, the missing leg, the scarred face, the grey hairs.

Perhaps you see the average man, and the average woman having zero ideas they have served your belated Queen and your Country.

Perhaps you have no idea that the effects of war have left that average man, that average woman broke.

Perhaps, you have no idea of the loud clacking of your car exhaust would cause a flashback, you in their faces being over friendly could cause some trigger in their mind and cause sensory overload and a PTSD attack.

That nightclub you would like your friend to come too… does not feel safe to your military veteran, there is too much noise, too many people, and too many chances for danger.

Or it may remind them of a busy street from Baghdad or Northern Ireland. Perhaps, you have no idea they are struggling.

You may think your friend is being rude when they say no, or shut off entirely, maybe, all they need is for you to understand and be patient with them.

Perhaps your husband or wife is having an outburst: being too emotional, too needy, too aggressive, too reserved, or they feel as though a massive elephant is sitting on their chest.

Perhaps they feel like they are suffocating. Perhaps they feel like their skin is crawling, perhaps they feel like their head is being shoved underwater.

Your Veteran wants to remove that elephant but they can't physically remove it on their own! they are generally screaming out for your support.

The elephant is getting heavier and it's crushing them, ''will you please help me move this elephant'' their ribs, heart, and chest is being squished, ''why can't you see the elephant?'

''Please, can you help me remove this elephant!'' ''Please be here for me''..'' I physically can't remove this elephant on my own.''

They need you to help them move the elephant off their chest!

Could you move an elephant off your chest alone?

It takes more than one person to move that elephant!

Support and your strength are needed.

Your Veterans' strength is being squished.

''I'm sorry I do not have the strength to do this alone,

I am sorry I need yours and I am making you tired too''

oh, they do feel like a burden to you, they feel in the way.

Yes, even without your help the elephant will soon want to move and the anxiety and pressure pass through your veteran is left bruised, exhausted, and tired.

And there certainly will be another elephant to come along for another quick rest!

For anxiety to come back around and sit on your veteran's chest.

Now the cycle repeats!

Though, the next time, the next time this elephant seems heavier than the one before.

crushing further down… is this because he or she is already bruised?

They haven't had enough time to heal or recover from the elephant before.

Please help your veteran remove that elephant in their chest.

Please help them recover so they are strong enough to handle the next one and please as a veterans partner, please do take some rest and recovery for you too.

You also do not want to get sat on by the elephant!

You also are important.

If you are a family member or a friend of a veteran who is suffering - please reach out to charities for support.

You are not alone!

If you see your veteran feeling suffocated or acting out of character please talk to them.

Please understand your normal, their old normal is now not normal.

That walk down a busy supermarket used to be a breeze, they were fine, happy, and content.

Still, on their good days they are still a breeze, but, on some days they are not, and some days that busy supermarket feels like the pits of hell.

they can't tell you which days!

They do not plan when it suddenly feels like hell.

It just happens.

You have to be prepared.

Today it could be a breeze for the first 30 minutes. then suddenly out of nowhere, they need to get out!

It's now hell.

you are confused- no idea why.

And they, your veteran.

The same.

They are confused and have no idea why.

They suddenly feel like they are in hell!

As much as you are confused and stressed so are they.

Some wounds you see, and some wounds are Invisible!

She or he is the tough veteran, a stand up man or guy.

They returned home from war.

No physical scratches and they seemed happy when they returned, though something slightly different.

Though, you could never put your finger on it. they may talk of the odd few incidents and laugh as if it was a joke and then suddenly years later, as you watch the light in their eyes fade, as you watch their sparkle disappear, and yet,

You have no idea why!

Well, they were okay when they returned from war, they weren't Injured and they were making light of their stories!

That was a copying mechanism they were in survival the reality of war hadn't yet kicked in.

You see, PTSD isn't always immediate, it comes on suddenly for e.g. when your partner becomes a parent and there are memories of war; children of their enemies, or killing a child's father for their own lives!

Yes, that's the harsh/awful/painful reality!

And now.
well now, reality has kicked in.
Guilt has kicked in.
PTSD has kicked in.

It could be a sudden smell, that they seemed unphased about before and wow that smell has triggered something, something they thought they long forgot!

It was never forgotten it was tucked down deep Inside their mind and now it's at the front!

It could be a date.. an anniversary of their colleague's passing.

It could be anything!

We all know about the five sensors.

Sight, Sound, Smell, Taste, Touch,

Well PTSD is triggered by any one of these!

An episode of PTSD can be caused by any of the five senses.

No, your veteran will not always know or be sure of what triggered them.

They may not even understand what's happening to them.

They may not realise they have PTSD!

But now one of those senses has activated a memory, an unhealed wound, the band-aid well
that just got ripped off, and now the wound you do not see, the wound inside their mind is bleeding.

One of those senses just ripped open that wound… you can't see it, you just see your veteran acting out of character.

Yet, they are internally bleeding!

Their mind is now catastrophic, their mind un-easy and having no idea what is happening to them!

They are confused!

Why are they here again?

Why are they at war again?

Why do they feel like they are surviving again? All you see is your beloved veteran, the same face, perhaps, just a different expression.

Same person, perhaps just a different tone in their voice.

The same smile, perhaps looking slightly altered.

Same hobbies, perhaps they have suddenly lost interest?

Same laugh, perhaps seemingly fake. Same banter, perhaps seemingly dark. Same outgoing friend, perhaps, seeing them less than you did before.

Perhaps, your veteran is internally bleeding from memories that keep seeping through their skin, through their eyes, through their ears, and through their mind!

Perhaps, your veteran can not switch off from these memories that are drowning them!

The memories that haunt them whilst they sleep, that haunt them through their waking hour. Perhaps, your veteran is feeling scared and alone and trapped inside their memories.

Guilt ridden by the life they couldn't save, the man, woman, or child they killed! Their friend, their brother or sister they couldn't protect.

Perhaps, your veteran is wishing they died on that battlefield, perhaps, your veteran wants the memories to stop and go back down.

Perhaps, your veteran Is tired of the torture pain and memories, and any sense that triggers them. Perhaps, you are tired too.

Perhaps they are filled with more guilt from the burden they feel they are putting on you.

And perhaps, our heroes, well they need a hero too!

Perhaps, you are that Friend, their wife their husband, their sister, their brother, their mother, their father.

Perhaps you are their hero?

Perhaps, you can be the veteran's hero?

How annoying is all the 'perhaps'- well that's like the mind repeating the same memory over and over)

You as family and friends have no idea how much you save our veterans' lives!

You save them over and over again!

You may not always feel like you listening/supporting makes you a hero, but you

are. You see your veteran as a hero but they, your veteran, see you as theirs.

Thank you to our veterans and thank you to those who support our veterans.

You are all remembered.

Thank you to our charities and our mental health teams that support our veterans.

What is PTSD?

What is PTSD?

Well PTSD - post-traumatic stress disorder!
A mental health condition that can occur immediately or years after a traumatic event and not just from war, you can also get complex PTSD you can experience more than one traumatic event which has affected you greatly!

Does PTSD ever go away: no is your answer, no it never goes away… however, with effective evidence based treatment, symptoms can be managed well and can remain doormats for years, even decades.

And there is a possibility for triggers at any apparent moment!

But NO, it never goes away!

PTSD symptoms:

Flashbacks to a traumatic event, nightmares, feeling extremely anxious, difficulty sleeping, intrusive thoughts.

Intense distress, an inability to connect properly with others, feeling detached or estranged from other people, isolation; anger outbursts, emotional outbursts, feeling sadness, feeling fear, or anger.

Physical sensations such as trembling sweating and nausea.

Mood changes, irritability, loss of memory, struggling to find words that were there a minute ago, forgetfulness; lack of motivation, changes in thinking pattern, hyper vigilant not feeling safe at all: a sense of impending doom, immediate danger depression, destructive behaviors, and the worst suicidal thoughts and actual suicide.
So we have some physical sides of PTSD

What does it feel like, physically?

Increased blood pressure and heart rate, fatigue, muscle tension, nausea, and joint pain. Headaches, back pain, and other types of pains.

PTSD is an anxiety disorder hence physical symptoms are similar to anxiety!

According to recent studies PTSD and emotional trauma can cause brain damage and physical damage.

PTSD does affect your sleep.

Perhaps struggling to fall asleep is restless insomnia and nightmares- a lack of sleep affects your daily living!

Ptsd can create memory loss as well as an impaired ability to learn new things what can trigger an episode attack of PTSD?

Stressful situations can trigger an attack If PTSD, a relationship break downs-feeling similar emotions, arguing, fighting, seeing things that remind you of the event, for e.g.

You were in a car crash in a red car a year later you see a car the same color and same make as the car you were in an accident in this could trigger a PTSD attack.

Smelling something that reminds you of this event.

The five senses!

If any of those are activated and ~~reminded of the~~ event it can trigger a PTSD attack.

When you encounter this trigger you will go through some of the symptoms above and you could end up having a panic attack or out bursting into violence or aggression and perhaps turn to a substance to ease the pain.

This could turn into self harming through substance abuse, eating disorders, cutting yourself, or in another damaging activity.

How to help someone with PTSD?

Be patient

Be supportive as those with PTSD are more likely to experience social isolation, and avoid family and friends.

The sense of isolation can sometimes worsen the symptoms practice being a steady and reliable and trustworthy person In their lives.. do not push them when they are not ready.

Listen
Do not judge
Show respect

Learn about their triggers and what PTSD is not all symptoms are what you may see in the movies, some are less subtle and you may just think your friend is just quieter than usual when they could be having a start of a PTSD attack, notice the little things like a slight shift in their behaviors or sound of their t voices.

Help them seek out help and encourage them too.

Learn about PTSD so you can understand more
and make sure you have support too, learnt to find ways for you to cope as their support
system you need to be okay too!

That's important.

What should you NOT say to someone with PTSD?

Just get over it they would if they could and they can't do not undermine their feelings and
what they are going through it's ten times what they are actually showing!

Do not belittle them like that, instead support them!

"People have been through worse"
"You're overreacting"
'But that was a long time ago"

"Things weren't that bad"
"My friend went through something similar and she
got over it"
"You're too sensitive"

"You just have to face your fears"

And many other belittling things you could say to undermine their feelings and make them
feel even more useless than they already feel.

There could even be trigger words that trigger them into an attack, try and find out what
words trigger them.

Also be aware a lot of people like to blame everything on the person with PTSD oh it's
your PTSD when in fact they may actually be reacting to a normal situation like a normal
person, please do not gaslight someone with PTSD.

Remember they are not stupid, they are intelligent men and women have respect for
them!

Do not use their mental health disorder as an ex issue to abuse them!

So now we have some facts about homelessness and PTSD.

Which is in turn why I am writing this short book.

Amber Guymer-Hosking.

The Veterans Pomes

BEE

In Norway's fretted coast today the ships of Hitler lie,
From cloud to cloud, the message ran, the watching eagle soared,
"The Bismark" and "Prince Eugen", have sailed from Bergen Fjord.
From cloud to cloud the answer flashed, now war is on the sea,
With find the foe and sink the foe, wherever they may be.
The dogs of war were off the leash, in snow and mist and gale,
And "Norfolk" found and "Suffolk" found....and finding held the trail.

The mist came down upon the sea, and day withdrew her light,
The quarry blessed the cloak of dark, the hunter cursed the night.
But when the red and level sun, the sky began to burn,
The Norfolk and the Suffolk, were like shadows on his stern.
The night rolled back across the sea, and to the west there stood,
Twice twenty thousand tons of steel, the colossus of the "Hood".
And by her side the "Prince of Wales". The hounds they then gave "Tongue",
Their voice across the waves, the old one and the young.
Through thirteen miles of quaking air the shell's screamed on their track,
The Bismark showed a blazing wound, then flung her fury back.
She hurled her fury at the Hood and split her to the keel,
And thirteen hundred men went down, within their tomb of steel.

Then like a cur that snaps and runs, the Bismark turned her tail,
But Norfolk clung and Suffolk clung relentless to her trail.
But watching eagles saw her slow, though her safety was at stake,
And Oil the life-blood of a shipways spilling in her wake.
They ran the quarry through the day till evening dulled the sky,
And the guns upon the Prince of Wales drew once a brief reply.
As from the north, the west , the south, new hunters joined the chase,
A vow was now within their hearts,....to sink or take disgrace,
Victorious put her hawks aloft, to fight him in the dark,
And one torpedo, deadly true, smashed home upon its mark.
But mist came down upon the sea to aid the deep dark night,
So Norfolk tracked and Suffolk tracked their quarry out of sight.

King George the fifth, the Home fleet brought from north in hot-foot haste,
Renown and all her escorts from south were not outpaced.
The call was running through the air, before the dawn was grey,
And Rodney and the Ramillies, from convoy's turned away.
The south and westwards ran the chase, all day and all the night,
Across the seas and from the skies, the watchers strained their sight.
Day came.....they tracked her...lost her,...but their reward was won,
The Bismark swinging east alone,...alone and on the run.

I The Sheffield set upon her heels, Ark Royals planes put out,
This the ship the "Hun" so often sank, put Gobbels word in doubt.
For this ship their lies so often sank...exacted now the price,
and twice torpedoed Bismark slowed, and reeled and circled twice.

She limped away, the night came down, but Sheffield kept in sight,
And Zulu, Maori, Cossack, came up eager for a fight.
And twice the long torpedo shots, hit foe that tried to flee,
And soon the mighty Bismark lay a beacon on the sea,

She stopped, ..then struggled on an hour,and when the daylight came,
The fleet closed in to make the kill, but Bismark still spat flame,
So Norfolk and the rest replied for "Hood" and "Jervis Bay",
Close on two thousand miles we came, to bring this "Bill" to pay.
But the end was near, the end was sure, and then came swift and soon,
The Dorset shire, avenged our dead, an hour before the noon.

Within a span of seven days, from find, to chase, to kill,
The pride of Hitlers navy,.. learned the strength of Britain's will,
Our guard is on the trackless wastes, that run from west to east,
Our watch is on the ships that bear the tools to beat the beast,
Our faith is in the men who make our trust an easy care,
Proclaim the need, the answer comes...............
Our Navy will be there.
"Bee"

A Solders Lament

A OLDER WHO SURVIVED THEWAR A FEW YEARS LATERWROTE THREE WORDS IN MEMORY OF HIS COMRADES WHO DIED THESE ARE HIS WORDS.

I awake from my sleep to hear the birds singing.
And the leaves on the trees rustling.
And also the smell of the flowers in the fields.
Then came the nightmares of years long ago.
When I heard the sound of the guns.
And the screams of men wounded and dying.
It was all because of man`s greed and jealously.
That this war was so tragically fought.
So man could gain his freedom.
From these who had denied them theirs.
Now all that is left are rows and rows.
Of headstones with the names of those who died.
And the wild flowers that survived growing.
So when you see these fields today remember.
All those brave men who gave you freedom.
Never forget them for what they did for you.
Remember them always and never forget them.
If you forgot them in the years to come
It will all have been in Vain.
And all your freedoms you will have lost.
Guard your memories every day and remember.
What those before you did remember them always.
For freedom from tyranny is the greatest gift.

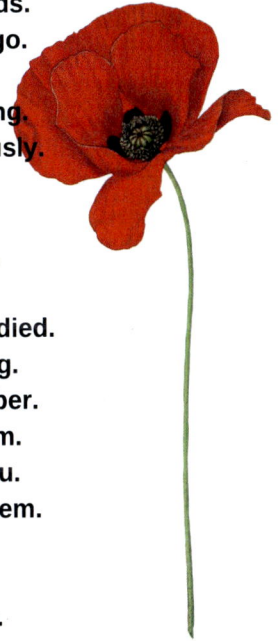

THANK YOU FOR LISTENING TO HIS WORDS BUT REMEMBER LIKE HIM NEVER FORGET THEM OR HIS WORDS WILL HAVE BEEN IN VAIN.

By J.A Thomason Veteran 15/19 Kings Royal Hussars

To the Corps

So here we sit, about to eat,
In the company of the elite,
We are brothers,
But not of the blood kind,
But we're strong in body,
Strong in mind.

Us men of green, stout of heart.
Have a glorious history, so where do I start?
Well at the beginning so now I'll impart,
A glimpse of our endeavours from the heart,

From our beginnings as the first Regiment of sea and land,
We set the standards working hand-in-hand,
From the musketry and grape fire at Bunker Hill,
To the glory of Trafalgar the enemy blood that spilled,

At Zeebrugge we launched ourselves into the fray,
The dragon slayer by our side on St Georges Day,
And then to Normandy an Invasion so bold,
The Commandos stormed ashore a sight to behold,

No weather defeats us the more severe we are at our best,
Be it sleet, rain wind or snow or the fiercest of tempest.

Onward to the Falklands and an Argentine stomp,
As well as fighting the enemy we showed the world how to yomp,
Now the troubles are over? They are in the past,
But for some of us here tonight, we will never forget a place called Belfast.

And into Iraq where this Unit did shine,
Saddam cowers by the lake now, that is our shrine,
And finally of course we mention that hell-hole of sand,
A place some here know, Afghanistan,
That valley of darkness that strikes fear within,
A shiver down my spine when I mention Sangin.

So 350 years we still stand at the fore,
We can conquer any land, terrain or shore.
If after these words you feel nothing inside?
Your hairs stand not up?
In you emotion does not reside?
Look in the mirror it is for you to decide,
Are your cold eyes empty? Or filled with a furnace of pride?

Finally remember those who have fallen, their bodies contorted their twisted
sinews destroyed,
Hold on to their memories and let their absence not be a void,
For theirs is the sacrifice that binds and unites the soul,
They will be remembered, their stories will be told!

We must honour them, savour them and cast out defamatory epithet,
Remember with great gladness, resist to lament,
To forget is unforgivable; apathy will be our regret,
Remember them always, for it is the doom of men that they forget.

Tribute to the 350th birthday of The Royal Marines.

By Michael Slunker

A Hero's Journey

It started many years ago,
With a birth of a double life,
A girl that would grow up to be,
Abused through out her life,

Her strength that would come from deep within,
And Would stay with her all life through,
Like when she was naughty and not so good,
While learning at her schools
As she got old enough to choose,
Which path in life to take,

While walking through a guarded gate,
An army rank to make,
Her training done 4 med to join,
Afghanistan the route,
Through casualties and babies cry's,

All done in blood stained boots,
The day did come she had to leave,
Eleven years service given,
PTSD was the parting gift,
The hell to see in vision,

They battled every day to find,
A place to lay there heads,
A home to feel safe at night
Instead of feeling dread.

Help for homeless veterans came,
From barnsley to pick up,
To get this hero on her feet,

Who never would give,
An ambassador now she's become,
For Help 4 homeless veterans
For Veterans who have to battle there way,
No more will they feel threatened

Written by Carl Pickersgil

Oh my goodness

" Oh my goodness your so lucky "
My friends would often say,
"To be dating a man in uniform,
Could you send his mates our way "

Little did they know what the uniform held beneath,
A story of destruction,
A tale of disbelief.
Appealing to the eye, this smartly dressed soldier,
Charming and so captivating
Respect he would upholder ?

But this was just the surface,
The sprinkle on the pie,
For what we were to go through,
This charming soldier and I.
A tale of love and war
The fine line between love and hate,
To try to fix or save him
I'm afraid was a little too late.

The voice he used in battle
Was often used at home,
The thousand mile stare
The mutterings when alone
You could say I was afraid?
Or maybe just in awe
This perfect looking soldier
Leaving gifts upon my door.

Being the partner of a service man
Whose mind was really lost
Was beyond my comprehension
And would come with such a cost.
I still salute this soldier
For all that he has done
But for me, the losing battle
Was to think we could be one

A soldier's partner- written by Anonymous

DAY OF REMEMBERANCE

As the light shines on another dawn,
On this remembrance day,
Our thoughts that return to yesteryear
With images of dread and fear,

It's about those men that stood their ground,
And the duties they had to do,
It's about the bullets going passed their heads,
And some going through and through,

They lost their lives at an amazing rate,
All to save our way of life,
The lucky ones got to fight some more,
With riffles guns and knife's,

They fought upon them foreign shores,
With all their guts and might.
They fought for all the families back home,
So we could sleep at night,
We will never grasp the horrors,

What our brave heroes had endured,
While fighting on them foreign shores
With freedom for their course
So please just take two minutes,

Of silence to stand still,
To remember all those fallen men
Who fought upon them hills?

Written By Carl Pickersgill

HE LONGEST DAY

Years ago we fought a war,
Was 6 of June we went ashore,
To stop the tyrants evil deeds,
Our soldiers fight had to succeed,
Our teams of men in crafts did load,

From ship to shore the men had flowed,
A hail of bullets they did meet,

Many thousand men feel from there feet,
The shore line came upon them fast,
Never know how many of them would last,
With trembling fear they all stood forth,
Awaiting landing on the shore,

The Landing craft doors open wide,
Onto the surging crimson tide,
Through bodies that were floating by,
Of all our heroes that had died,
This was the longest day for war,

Were we fought foes upon there shore,
Our men did triumph in the end,
So we could live and not pretend,

So give two minutes of silence please,
For men that fell upon their knees,
So we could live and just be free,
That's all of us including me,

Written By
Carl Pickersgill

Brother in Arms

One of our brothers, serving our nation
Taken away, as a sick demonstration.
He went for a walk, but nobody knew
What would become, what was waiting in
lieu.

Taken from us, in the most brutal way
Left in the street, whilst the murderers
play.
Passers by, saw the drama unfold
With the mobile phones, where the story
was told.

Our Great Nation, pulling together
Taking on extremists, to rid them forever.
Justice must serve, to send out a sign,
That mess with us, you've crossed the
line!

RIP Lee Rigby

Written by Matt Slater

Decision

A decision made as a child,
to serve your Country proud,

Signing on the dotted line,
an oath that you have vowed

To protect your Queen and Country,
whatever be the cost

Prepared to be a hero,
with the fallen comrades lost

It takes a type of person,
to do what we all do

To become a serving soldier,

to live, to serve,

Thank You.

Written by Matt Slater

What Caused Their Pain

Some days are good and some are not so good trying to understand
The depths of their struggle and dealing with their past all go hand in hand
Wanting to help them free their mind and help them come to grips with what
caused their pain

Hoping that one day they will believe that peace can ultimately be gained
It is not an easy road to travel and you cannot fix what has already occurred

All you can do is move forward with them with patience and a positive word
Unconditional love is a must and not to be taken lightly or with a grain of salt

Letting them know you are here and reassuring them what has happened is not
their fault

Do not pressure them with a million questions about when where how or why

That does absolutely nothing but make them push you away and not even want
to try

Listening to them and being silent as they speak is one very important fact
Allowing them to confide in you and rebuild trust that so many people tend to
lack
I am describing what life is like being a spouse of a Veteran who suffers with
PTSD

You better believe they are worth every tear you have cried and every
milestone that makes them a little more free

Written by Paula Gentry-Evenson

The Armoury

Here's my weapon Sir, I have cleaned it through.
The sights are set and it fires true.
Can I hand it in please so I can drive home?
It's Friday afternoon and I'm looking to roam.

No need to ask. Please lay down your gun.
You need it no longer, you are free my Son.
But please inspect so I know it is clean?
I know my place in this fighting machine!
It cannot be dirty, nor rusty or bent.
For when the time comes, my soul I have lent.
It must be ready.
It must fire true!
For it must kill those, who would kill me and you?

Settle down Soldier, your weapon is clean.
It's time for your mind to play all that you've seen..
The weapon is gone.
You need it no more, for your soul left your body on a foreign floor.

You are now free from you earthy chores.
Now go see your Siblings..

On Valhalla shores.

Written by Kev Walker

In Early April I Left Your Base.

They were rehearsing a soldiers funeral,
With pomp and grace,

On the way back,
I felt alone and stressed,
I felt faint and dizzy,
Weak and depressed,

I feared the taliban would take your life,
Far away with gun and knife,
My mind was blank but filled with fright,
Strange dreams filled my every night,

I couldn't protect you anymore,
In that far-away foreign shore,
But oh my daughter, you returned changed,
Experiences, your mind had re-arranged.

Written by Sarah Guymer

In Arduis Fidelis

Serpent and staff,
This was the cap badge,
Or your medical craft,

Desert type armour,
Combat boots: colour of sand,
Hard, tan helmet,
New squaddie tan,

This is my memory,
Of your time on tour,
The last thing I saw,
When you closed that front door,

The taxi took you to the train,
Then Brize Norton,
Packed of on a plane,
I hope that I will see you again.

Written by Sarah Guymer.

Remembrance Sunday.

Today Civilian or Soldier, we stand tall, chests out, shoulder to shoulder,
Looking around us, remembering only few grew older,

Wearing medals and poppies on the left of our chest,
Standing silent for two,remembering those we lay to rest.

Feeling a sense of pride with our brothers and sisters in arms,
Whilst part of our minds return to what harms,

Beret on our heads, families, friends and comrades by our side,
Laughing, joking, hiding that this morning we cried,

Some see us as mean, killing, tattooed machines, heartless even rude,
Some see, heroes of the land, peace keepers, a cool dude,

Some judge our service, wanting rid of today, hating on our patriotic pride,
But together we stand, a kingdom strong, side by side,

Most seem to forget those stood tall, lost a brother just yesterday,
You judge easily, because peace, love and a hero is what we need today!

Written by Amber Guymer-Hosking

The Homeless Veteran

They reach to us for help
The military they've left
But now all alone they feel bereft.
Well the help is here
now they've asked

We step in and lift them up
now that we've been tasked.

Rents bonds beds and care
Once linked to us
They're halfway there.

Lives turned around
Feet back on the ground
A sense of purpose and
a fresh future abound.

Help 4 Homeless veterans
A charity run by veterans
For veterans.

Written by Steve Bentham - Bates.

From the trenches to the deserts

To look at he's just a boy
With hopes and dreams just like us all
But through the gaze of a boy hood wonder lay a fate to a man like no other

He backs his bags with a half grin smile
But knowing he will be gone for quiet a while.

To him it's just a job fighting for his country in the Mob.

Don't make no mistake fear will kick in he's just a boy in a mans skin.

From the trenches to the deserts these boys will go, some never to return and
now you know.

They give their lives so you can yours.
Without a doubt in their mind of course

Remember them the fallen the brave,
Save a place above your heart place a poppy on the mark.

Remember them
Remember Them

With every grain of sand

With every grain of sand
Comes a new challenge
Anger controlling the way
Unable to sleep
Unable to speak

Feelings lock in a bottle of emotion
A broken former soldier
To many barriers
Locked up tight

Can't control what's inside
Raised angry voices
Scared daughters
A broken former soldier
Afraid to lose control
Fighting what's inside
Help is out there
To combat the stress
To mend what is broken

To Fix the broken former soldier
Whispers in the Dark

Deep in thought as I close my eyes
Knowing your right there by my side
Still unable to shift this feeling
A feeling so dark so low.
In the dark, whispers that I long to hear.
Travel through and disappear
Still I feel so alone inside
Even with you by my side.
Whispers in the Dark they come and go.
The light is love and it won't say no.
Help me through i know you will

True to me you remain still.
Where the sun meets the sand

Where the sun meets the sand
Is where a part of me remains
A mind now stuck not knowing what it is to be me.
Angry emotional broken and no one able to see
Where the sun meets the sand
Is where a part of me remains
The wounds of war not all visible to see
The agony of life beats you inside
Where the sun meets the sand
Is where a part of me remains
Embarrassed negative weak
The darkness smothers you to tears
Where the sun meets the sand

Is where a part of me remains

By Granite zeros

Just A Number

Back then you wasn't a name
Just a number
But you was so much more
A solider, A sailor An Airman
With a Warrior spirit
Putting your own life at risk for that of the people at home
A purpose
A smartly pressed uniform
A sense of overwhelming pride
A proud serving member of an elite group.
Beeming smiles as medals are pinned on your chest

Now
your just you.
That sense of pride accomplishment when you lace up your new work boots isn't
there.
The purpose you once had is fizzling away!
You wake up and feel lost.
All you want is to wear the uniform, shape that beret on your head and stand to
attention.
Have orders barked in your face.

However long you wait, that longing will last forever, it is in the past.
And in your mind you think
what is left, war story's and a veterans badge.
In reality your so much more, your the man your kids will look up to with wide
eyes and tell all their friends my Daddy is a veteran he went to war, he's a hero.
The man who's wife holds tight because she doesn't want to let u go.
And in those moments a glimmer of hope.

Your not just a number, your not just a badge.

You're a husband a Father, a friend a veteran

By Granite zeros

The Veterans Poems by Kids

War poem

The tank is green
Where has it been?

The poppy is red
For so many dead.

Soldiers are brave
For all that they gave.

The soldiers in heaven,
We'll never forget them.

The battle is hard
And many are scarred.

My mum is brave, for her boss had an end.

Belle age 6

I Wanted

One day I heard a jet plane,
So loud in the sky,
Mum saw that I was worried and explained the reason why,
"It's ok my darling, you have no reason to fear,
they're just testing out the planes from the camp base that is near,"

I wanted to believe her,
I want her to be right,
But what if war is coming
And it's on its way tonight?

I see the news on TV and I have to block my ears,
Not because I do not care,
But because these are my care free years.

I know that I am lucky
I know that I have to need to fear,
But when I hear those jet planes
I feel like War is near.

Stan age 12

The son of two war heroes.

My Mum and Dad gave up their freedom to war,
They returned alive, but something inside them, a roar,

I see them sometimes hidden in the dark and cry alone,
I'm there baby but now I'm nearly grown,

I wish I could do more to help,
Both of their war pains I have felt,

The life with two parents from war,
Moving house, meeting new people, my Mum says it's a new place to explore,

It's hard for an Army child too,
Goodbye and hello to new friends and houses and you,

I've lived a life not a normal child would understand,
I try, I do, but sometimes it's hard living in no man's land,

War took a piece of my parents from me,
The price they paid you can't all see,

I'm More then just a son of two war heroes.
I'm the son of my two heroes and I'm their hero too.

Written by Brandon Casey Aged 12

**In memory of our
Men and Woman**

**Who where left on the
battlefield**

The reality of conflicts in Afghanistan.

We will remember you.

We will remember you.

Operations in Afghanistan

This is the reality of how many soldiers we lost in one war zone on the battlefield.

This is not the list of those who have since committed suicide from their conflict in Afghanistan.
Over the last 20 years of deployment in Afghanistan, there have been 457 deaths of UK armed forces personnel. The number of fatalities peaked between 2009 and 2010 when over 100 personnel were killed. Of the total 457 personnel who died whilst on deployment to Afghanistan 405 died because of hostile action.

During Operation Herrick, the codename for which all British military operations were conducted from 2002 to 2014, there were 616 serious or very serious casualties among armed forces and civilian personnel. As with deaths, these casualties peaked in 2009 and 2010.

There were a total 7,807 field hospital admissions, although most admissions were related to disease or a non-battle injury. Around 28% (2,209) of admissions to field hospitals were those wounded in action.

Additionally, there were 7,477 medical air evacuations during the 12-year operation.

We will remember all of you who have lost your lives on the battlefield and the ones who lost their battle at home once returning from the battlefield.

Since 1945, the deadliest year for the British Armed forces was 1951, when there were 851 operational deaths. This was due to three separate conflicts: the Malayan Emergency, the 1951 Anglo-Egyptian War, and the Korean War. Between 1959 and 2009 there were only three years that had more than 100 operational deaths: 1972, 1973, and 1982. The spike in deaths in the early 1970s was the result of the political violence in Northern Ireland at the time, and 237 of the 297 deaths in 1982 happened during the Falklands War. Over this period there have been a total of 7,192 British military deaths in conflicts.

Who lost their lives on active duty for their Country and their Families.

We will remember you.

Over 145 thousand personnel in 2020
The British Armed Forces are composed of four separate branches, the British Army, the Royal Navy, the Royal Air Force, and the Royal Marines. Of these branches, the British Army has more personnel than the other three combined at over 82 thousand. The Royal Air Force had around 33 thousand personnel, the Navy at over 27 thousand, and the Marines 6.64 thousand amounting to 145 thousand overall.

The Royal British Legion's long-held estimate is that somewhere between three and six percent of homeless people have an armed forces background, but there are concerns that some homeless veterans are rendered "invisible" by the way statistics are collected.
In a 2014 report surveying the ex-forces community, the Legion reported that the number of veterans living on the streets in London has plummeted since the 1990s when figures indicated that 20 percent of the homeless population was ex-services at the time. A 2008 study found that the proportion had dropped to six percent.

More recent statistics suggest that rough sleeping among veterans is at an even lower rate in the present day. The Combined Homelessness and Information Network, known as CHAIN, track the flow of rough sleeping in London and is regarded as one of the most accurate measures in the UK, ahead of the official annual counts.

The database revealed the percentage of UK nationals with experience serving in the armed forces was as low as three percent in 2017/18 and fell to two percent in 2018/19. And the percentage remained the same for 2019/20 with 129 UK veterans seen by outreach workers sleeping rough. When foreign nationals are taken into account, six percent of people sleeping rough in 2019/20 had served in the armed forces at some point in their lives.

But the London-centric nature of the figures demonstrates just one of the problems with counting how many veterans are homeless across England and the wider UK.
In early 2020, the University of Salford academic Mark Wilding penned a report on the subject which found that veterans were "predominantly self-referring into direct access hostels or accessing support through Armed Forces charities and community organizations" rather than going through the statutory homelessness system.

The problem with the statistics the way that they are is it renders homeless veterans invisible.

This is backed up by statistics showing the number of veterans approaching councils for help with homelessness in England between April and June 2019. A total of 70,030 households were assessed and owed a prevention or relief duty – when the council is required to step in to prevent or relieve homelessness under the Homelessness Reduction Act – but only 440 were recorded as needing support due to serving in the armed forces, making up 0.63 percent of the figures.

We will remember you.

While reporting to armed forces charities is not problematic in itself, with ex-servicemen and women able to access specialist support, Wilding suggested that some homeless veterans were being rendered "invisible" in statistics.

He said: "It shouldn't necessarily be the case that you have to go the statutory homelessness route because veterans often have specialist issues that the local
authority homelessness team might not be best equipped to cope with.

"It should be that they can get that support from armed forces charities, especially if they are best placed to help them, but this needs to be recognized. Because beyond the knowledge of these armed forces charities who are doing that work, it becomes quite separated from homelessness as a mainstream issue.

"The charities are doing that work but this is the problem with the statistics in the way that they are – it renders homeless veterans invisible."

Wilding insisted that there needs to be a change in how homelessness statistics are collected to improve coverage, suggesting that replicating the CHAIN model
elsewhere would benefit how we understand not only rough sleeping but the scale of veterans living on the streets.

A greater take-up of the Armed Forces Covenant – a promise by the nation ensuring that those who serve or who have served in the armed forces, and their families, are treated fairly – among housing organisations could also help to join up the work being already done to combat homelessness among veterans.

The academic added: "It's pretty difficult to get to the crux of the problem. It would require the government to change the way that homelessness statistics are collected because they are based on priority need. So in that sense, homelessness statistics are an underestimate of what's actually out there.

"There's definitely scope for bottom-up work to be done. The work that CHAIN does is supported by the London Mayor so perhaps if other regions were able to get that support from the local government then they could do similar things.

And help to try and get attention to the issue."

Conflicts of the British Amy

1 Roman Invasion & Conquest (55 BC-96 AD)

·2 Viking & Anglo-Saxon Invasions (5th-10th Centuries)

·3 Norman Conquest & Subsequent Conflicts (1066-1071; 12th century)

·4 Barons' Wars (1215-1217; 1264-1267)

·5 Hundred Years' War(1337-1453)

·6 War of the Roses (1455-1487)

·7 Anglo-Spanish War (1585-1604)

·8 Wars of the Three Kingdoms (1639-1653)

·9 Seven Years' War

·10 The American Wars

·10.1 Queen Anne's War (1702-1713)

·10.2 War of the American Independence (1775-1783)

·10.3 War of 1812 (1812-1814)

·11 Napoleonic Wars & Resulting Conflicts (1803-1815)

·11.1 Anglo-Russian War (1807-1812)

·11.2 Anglo-Swedish War (1810-1812)

12 Anglo-Afghan Wars (1839–1842; 1878–1880; 1919)

·13 Crimean War (1853–1856)

Conflicts of the British Amy

14 The Boer Wars (1880-1881; 1899-1902)

·15 The Great War (1914-1918)

·16 World War II (1939-1945)

·17 The Cold War (1947-1991

Northern Ireland,

First second and third Cod war

The troubles 1968-1998

Aden Emergency 1963-1967

Indonesia -Malaysia conflict 1963-1966

The Falklands,1982

Iraq,

Lebanon 1982-1984

The gulf war 1990-1991

Bosnian war
Operation desert fox
Kosovo war
Sierra Leone
Libyan war
Operation shader
Persian gulf crises

To Summarize

We have talked about the reality, the facts, the feelings.. took a look inside the minds of our veterans and looked as some harsh realities.

This book has been created to spread awareness, to raise money towards Help4homeslessveterans

And yo raise the knowledge of PTSD and Homelessness in the United Lingdom.

Please if you feel effected by anything in this book please ensure you reach out for
help or support and get support.

PTSD is not just for soldiers, civilians can get this too.

Please everybody, think of one thing you like about your self today? Think about one thing you achieved today.

Think about your dream/Goal.. and what would your first small task be to help achieve your dream?

Please find five minutes to just move your body around and step into the sunshine. Please create positivity and encourage others to be positive.

Namaste

Thank you for your support.

Kind regards.
Amber Guymer-Hosking

Supporting
Help 4 Homeless Veterans

**Charity Number: 1148155 |
Registered in England and Wales**

Printed and bound by CPI Group (UK) Ltd, Croydon, CR0 4YY

08/02/2024

03692610-0001